# Abba
# Hear My Prayers

*for times I cannot pray myself*

*Blessings*

*Peggy McMahon*

*Peggy McMahon*

Publication
Consultants
Since
1978

*I dedicate this book to
my husband Brian,
my son Sean, and my daughter Katherine.
Thank you Abba for placing them
in my love and in my life.*

*~ Introduction ~*

This is a book about hope. It is about God's grace, his love and his forgiveness.

I began writing this book as my prayer journal during an extended illness, and it has become an embracing story about life's journey and our search for meaning and purpose. We all pass through times of pain and suffering when we may feel spiritually bereft and isolated, times when the words of prayer elude us, or are so deep within us we cannot reach them.

Although God knows my every thought and need, I find it comforting to come to Him with prayers upon my lips, prayers of praise and thanksgiving, as well as petitions for help and deliverance. I believe my prayers come through the Holy Spirit as I allow my mind to open, my hand to write, and my spirit to answer, "Yes, Lord."

The prayers in this book are organized by the days of the week, but you may choose to read them in any order. You may want to use this book like a daily devotional or you may want to seek out the prayers that speak to your heart. The book starts on an ordinary Thursday when I began to speak daily with God about my illness. Through the reading and writing of God's word I am learning to offer my illness as a gateway to the divine, knowing that our Father's word never comes back void and empty.

It is my hope that these prayers will have a universal appeal and will be prayed by seekers and new believers, as well as by those who are living a life of quiet communion with God. You may want to pray alone in the sacredness of your own heart, or in groups seeking connection with God and with one another. At times you may find you are praying in the light of Christ's presence, at other times you may be on your knees in the isolating darkness of struggle and doubt.

My prayers reach out to all people who thirst for a more intimate relationship with God.

I would especially like to send my prayers to my sisters around the world, for we have much in common. We are faced with spiritual struggle no matter where we are. We can lean into it, or we can try to run away. Our journey is not complete until we take it in and give it back. Whatever is naturally occurring, whether it is pain, illness, grief or suffering, we then need to offer what we have learned, for others to use as a stepping stone in their own journey. So I pass on to my sisterhood these prayers from my heart, reminding myself that I am not in charge of the harvest, I am just in charge of the planting.

My prayer for us all is from Isaiah 30:21. *Whether you turn to the right or to the left, your ears will hear a voice behind you saying, This is the way; walk in it.*

*Amen.*

*Peggy*

Daily Prayers
for living in Faith and
for touching the heart of my Soul

∝
Come Thirsty

*You received God's spirit when he adopted you as his own children. Now we call him, Abba, Father.*

Romans 8:15 New Living Translation

## ~ *Thursday* ~

Father, Father,

You, who hear the awful groaning of my soul, carry me I pray, through one more day. Lift me in your precious arms, let my tears wash over me as you feed my soul. Let me drink the water as one who is thirsty for life. Touch my heart and fill my longing with your peace. Love me. Rest, help me rest. *Amen.*

## ~ *Friday* ~

Most gracious and loving Father,

You have gifted me with those who are willing to stand by me and I am grateful. Without their strength, I would fall; without their compassion, I would wither. There are days and nights when the ocean is so wide that I am unable to swim its breadth. It is then, they keep me afloat. It is then, they listen to my breath with their soul, and they breathe life for me.

In this circle of existence, I am, because they are. Thank you for the gift of your children, who help this child to survive. *Amen.*

## ~ *Saturday* ~

My Father,

Protect me with shelter today, I pray. Shield me from the icy winds of anguish, from blinding storms of doubt; draw aside the black curtain of despair and let me walk in the light of your love.

Open my mind to all that is positive. Turn me from the well worn tracks of self-defeating thoughts. Bathe my troubled mind with redolent spirit. Nourish me like a child of the water, a child of the truth.

Let me rest upon your arms, until my breath flows quiet into the sea.

*Amen.*

## ~ *Sunday* ~

Most Holy Father, Giver of all life,

On this holy day of communion, I come to your house frail and trembling. My soul has been bruised, I need you. Touch me with the oil of your Spirit, mend my brokenness. Help me believe that for what I ask, you have already given. I need not be perfect, I need only to have faith.

*Amen.*

O Blessed Father,

This day has come and gone and I am learning patience. And with patience comes peace, although for me not easily.

Teach me how easy it is to trust you, so that I never again have to wrestle the bearer of ambivalent fear. Let me know that you have already wrestled him for me and you know the outcome. Let me feel your faith in me, so that I might be strengthened.

Is it really so difficult I ask, and you answer, "Most assuredly not."

Father, if you walk in front, I will follow, if you walk beside, I will lean into you. If you walk behind I will fall back on you. No matter where I am, there you will be. I am not alone. Teach me this, I pray.

*Amen.*

### ⊃ *Reflection* ⊂

*Thou preparest a table before me in the presence of mine enemies: thou anointest my head with oil, my cup runneth over. Surely goodness and mercy shall follow me all the days of my life; and I will dwell in the house of the Lord forever.*

Psalm 23:5-6 KJV

O Holy Spirit,

My body is so bone tired, yet my soul longs for you. I long for you to take me to the place where all pain is no more, all anxiety and sadness gone. Show me, I pray, how to use my pain for strength, as a doorway to faith.

Let me lie down with the assurance that all is right with me, that all is part of your intended plan.

Lie me down under your star studded sky, give me your promise that you will rest beside me tonight, watching over me as I sleep. Remind me that all I need do is to believe and you will do the rest.

Help me break through the waves of pain and torment. Show me an ocean at rest so that I might know how vast is your peace. And in the morning, shower me with warm sun in the midst of this winter, delight me with birdsong outside my window.

Be ever my guardian and keep me safe from harm.
*Amen.*

∝ *Reflection* ⋈

*Whatever you ask for in prayer, believe that you have received it and it will be yours.* Mark 11:24

## ~ Wednesday ~

My dear Father,

The tempest winds blow over the edge of my mind today. Not howling rages, but enough to distract my thoughts, enough to take me away from you.

Please touch me, bring me back to you. Let me feel your healing hand across my timid mind. Let me feel I belong. Bless my precious friend, hold her in your loving embrace. May I stand beside her, as she has stood beside me countless times. Bless us both, give us peace.

*Amen.*


## ~ Thursday ~

My Father,

Let my hunger be satisfied in you, my thirst be quenched. When I stumble be there to hold me, when I tire be there to replenish, when I reach the end be there.

The wind blows today, the cold pierces my skin, yet I feel this unbelievable warmth that comes from inside me, because I know you have kindled the fire of my desires even before I was born. How can I not believe in you? There is proof all around me. The snowflakes displaying their unique design, the blue of the sky giving way to limitless color, the compatibility of my special friend, whom you sent to comfort me.

How can I doubt you? In all your creative ways teach me faith.

*Amen.*

## ~ *Friday* ~

Loving Father,

A crashing despair has depleted my reserves. All hope seems lost. Please hold me close, comfort me and point me in the direction I am to go. Be with those who use their minds to reach mine. Let me know that this too shall pass and that this "fellowship of little people together make God visible in the world."( *Can You Drink The Cup*, Henri Nouwen)

I want to believe that truth, yet the rawness of this pain is still too frightening for some. Guide me to those who have looked straight into this fear and persevered. Perhaps that is all we can ask....just help to persevere.

*Amen.*

## ~ *Saturday* ~

O Holy God,

I pray for transcendence. I pray for flight above and beyond this troubled mind. You, who know everything, and fulfill all pleas for peace, restore my dignity, not just for me, but so that I may serve you with honor and respect.

Turn my mind from self-indulgent, selfish thoughts and ask me—no, command me, escort me, carry me out of the darkness into the light.

*Amen.*

## ~ *Sunday* ~

Most gracious and loving Father,

I ask you to hold my cup of sorrow Lord, until I am strong enough. Then slowly, surely show me how to lift it. For now, hold my anxious mind in your cupped hands. Still the noise in the rapid turbulence of my heart so that I might pray in the inner chapel of my soul. Let the silence of your word transform my burdensome thoughts.

Teach me how to ask for your presence, then show me how to listen with my soul. Bring me to that place where joy and sorrow embrace each other. Bring me peace for the night. *Amen.*

## ~ *Monday* ~

Oh weary head, I want rest. Turn my heart toward you Father. Hold me as you would a little child. Soothe my fears, still my hand, slow my thoughts. Lead me to your psalms, you who provide rest in green pastures and respite beside still waters.

Help me understand that you are waiting, that all I need do is to look within. You wait for me inside.

As one who has wept in loneliness with the fear of being separated from you O Father, turn to me, let me know that you are not outside in the world of emotions. Assure me that you are waiting inside for me; all I need is to ask you to be with me and you are there.
*Amen.*

## ~ *Tuesday* ~

Loving Father,

Fatigue is heavy on my soul… as if a thousand battles have been fought in just one day. Getting better sometimes simply means just not giving up. Stay close to my side today. Still these furtive urges to give up that are born from an overwhelming bone-tiring fatigue. It is then that I wonder how I can stay.

Fight this one for me Father. If not for me, then with me. I ask this in the name of your Son, who fought the biggest battle of all. Mine does not compare.

*Amen.*

## ~ *Wednesday* ~

Dear Lord,

As we move nearer to Easter, help me connect to the story. Teach me that I cannot always rely on my feelings. Chase off all messengers of greed who wait to deliver me to the doubters. I cannot now, afford to keep company with doubt.

Help me understand that by accepting my suffering I can look upon grace with new eyes. And you will always, always have a place for me.

*Amen.*

## ~ Thursday ~

O Lord,

I am treading on dangerous ground. I beg of you, turn my mind to giving thanks for life and your blessings. Still my heart, give me comfort. I feel besieged and I want to give up. Where are you taking me God? I long for respite. Take me into the dark of night and walk me through to the other side. I cannot do this alone, please help me.

*Amen.*

## ~ Friday ~

My Father, my Father,

There is no father in flesh who can deliver me from this pain. I know this. Help me turn again to you for help. Let my apology for my weakness transcend my tears and become a petition for your strength. I am so well aware that I cannot do this alone.

At times I rail against you, ranting that you've done enough to bring me to my knees. Yet I know I have to stand up again. Help me, while on bended knee, look up to find the brilliance of your light surrounding me. Help me turn around to find you walking behind me, your cloak of armor at the ready. At the ready for me, for my protection. For me, you would do this for me. There have been prayers more eloquent, but I am here to stand for authenticity. There is so little left of me and so much for me to gain from you. Welcome me now. Welcome me.

*Amen.*

Father, Father,

Gaze at me with eyes of forgiveness. I stumble, I fall, I get up. The day follows the moon into night; you protect me in sleep from dusk to dawn. One step forward, my feet keep moving. Instill in me the will to live. Lift me out of the shadow that lies across my being.

Reassure me that my body is sufficient to carry all the awareness you have presented me. At times I want to beg of you to take it back, saying, "It's too much, it's too heavy." If I am part of the fire in the crucible, give me courage to burn brightly as you tenderly lift me beyond the flames.

Most of all, Father, I pray for courage. Let me stand and face the dusky demons who tend the harvest and raise the power of self-accusation. Let me call on the name of your Son, Jesus, who holds all power and glory, to dispel the darkness, and lead me into the light. *Amen.*

### ⚮ *Reflection* ⚮

*The Lord upholds all those who fall and lifts up all who are bowed down.* Psalm 145:14

*~ Sunday ~*

My Father, My Father,

I feel such a failure tonight. While others hurt, I stand by weeping in self-pity. I plead with you to pull me out of self-indulgence. I feel neither righteous nor brave tonight, only broken and sinful.

If I am clay, already you are speaking to my inner shape. If I am clay then there must be hope for me. Clay is mud, it is simple, it is supple, it is pliant; it begs for shape. Its potential is limited only by the master's hand, which has no limits. Clay is patient. Clay waits for me to listen to the master's plan, which is at my heart center. It is there that you bring my potential to light. It is there that you fill my empty aching heart with God shaped potential.

Clay has character and is unique. It is limited only by the master's flawless design and creativity. If I am clay, teach me daily, hour by hour, minute by minute how to place my desires on hold and to listen to the potter mold me into universal creation. *Amen.*

## ◇ *Reflection* ◇

*For You formed my inward parts; You wove me in my mother's womb. I will give thanks to you, for I am fearfully and wonderfully made; wonderful are your works, and my soul knows it very well. Psalm 139:13-14 NASB*

## ~ *Monday* ~

Father God,

Thank you God for reminding me that I need not be perfect, that I only need to be willing.

Willing first of all to slow down. Willing to listen to your whispers, God, in the branches of my soul; willing to say yes when my whole being sees nothing but a void.

Show me the strength of your vine and how no branch is left unsupported. Make the supports visible to my eye if I need more substance to my faith. As a master gardener, show me the fruit from your carefully tended branches. Reveal to me the garden of life, with its victories and setbacks, weeds and butterflies, all collected in the same small plot, which is my story.

Ultimately, bring me to my knees in grateful adoration for all you have done for me.

*Amen.*

## ~ *Tuesday* ~

Father,

The rising sun presents a challenge to me each morning. A challenge to carry its light and its warmth far into the day and to hold on to the memories through the night. Hold me to my aspirations, God—to be able to sit in a place of stillness and allow you the opportunity to work in me. Give me peace, I pray. Help me stop my bids for control and power, null my stretches for perfection through my own wisdom and judgment.

*Amen.*

## ~ *Wednesday* ~

Blessed Father,

I give thanks for a daughter who is a blessing to behold. Her inner and outer beauty sing the lyrics of your spirit. In the lilac of spring she blossoms, in the navy of night she shines. I cherish each moment with her. I ask the Father's Son to proclaim that the doubter's shadow has no authority over this mother and daughter of Love.

We are free to walk in the light. We are liberated to be free of fear. I pray for strength for tomorrow and for safety for me and my daughter.

*Amen.*

## ~ *Thursday* ~

Loving Father,

I fall on my knees in gratitude that you have blessed me with a son who carries not only the strength of your word, but also the tenderness of your love which he cradles in his heart.

It is he who sheds tears upon my suffering, praying that I may be healed. It is he who has also travelled this dusty road and I pray for his protection.

I ask the Father's Son to proclaim that the doubter's shadow has no authority over this mother and son of love. Keep us from harm.

*Amen.*

## ~ Friday ~

Father, Father,

Oh how I long for your embrace, the loneliness of this world pierces my heart at times, and yet I do know that the constancy of your love ever surrounds me. Although I do not always "feel" your love, help me to know that it is real, true and infinite.

There are times when my soul yearns to leave this exhausted body, to transcend this corporeal existence and dance with universal stars. Oh what joy to fly with the Angels, to know only peace, to be bathed in love, not tears. Let me listen to the whisperings of my heavenly lover.

*Amen.*

## ~ Saturday ~

My Abba,

The tenderness of this endearing name brings tears to my eyes for I know that even in my faintest calling of you, Abba, I have nothing less than your full attention.

The more I pray, the more I want to pray. I find myself more vulnerable, yet more secure, weaker yet full of strength, empty handed, yet full at heart. I am aware that this tempering of your precious child has purpose and meaning. I feel it deep down in the marrow of my bones, a purposeful mystery. Will I recognize the part I am to play in the oil of your painting? How will you use me?

*Amen.*

## ~ Sunday ~

O Protector God,

I ask you to descend upon my body and keep me safe from harm. Enter the portal to my soul and summon your guardian Angels to watch over me. Keep them ever vigilant so that I may lay down in peace. Cloak them with your armor so that they may banish the evil one and keep him far from me. Let him be rejected, never accepted.

I acknowledge that I am in a fight for my life and that I am not of sufficient strength to be my own defender. I pray that you bear me up on eagle's wings and help me win the fight, knowing that only you can deliver me.

*Amen.*

## ~ Monday ~

Dear Father,

I feel the blessings of your most Holy word. You have stilled my mind, removed the turbulence from my heart, and given me peace. For this I am so very grateful. For now you have banished the voices of doubt and self-accusation and given me instead your steady word of assurance.

I rest on the sea of your tranquility. I drink of the river of your mercy and eat of the fruit of your love. There is nothing I need that you have not provided. I pray that you hear all heartfelt prayers, spoken and unspoken, and answer as you have answered me. Thank you.

*Amen.*

## ~ Tuesday ~

O my God,

I feel I need a mother tonight and so I will pray to you, both Mother and Father of all children. Wipe these tears from my face, touch me with the softest whisper of consoling grace. Rock me in your embrace, sing to me the songs of Angels, and praise my efforts at faith.

Help me pray my way into full faith, knowing that as I kneel, you have already answered my prayer. Oh, to have that much faith…..it would be joyful, exhilarating. And yet, it is not complicated, indeed it is quite simple. *Ask and it will be given to you; seek and you will find; knock and the door will be opened to you.* Matthew 7: 7

Help me find what it is that I am seeking, even when I do not know what it is myself.

Bless me, ease my suffering, let me feel your love, and spirit me though this most difficult day.
*Amen.*


## ~ Wednesday ~

O my Lord,

How thoughtful is your presence, when my own thoughts are racing. Hold me steadfast to the promise you have made to me and I to you. Still my mind, still my heart. You, only you, know this almost unbearable struggle I am in. No other can know it as you know it. Therefore, I am not alone.

Cover me with the warm leaf blanket of spring, open my skin to the healing rays of the sun. Guide my feet to the right path and give me courage to stay the journey.

For all those in this world who are today struggling with the decision to go on, make that decision for them. Life is good. It is a gift from you that we accept, not reject. Keep us all safe.

*Amen.*

## ~ *Thursday* ~

O Holy God,

Holding on to you is my strength, O Lord; make me strong, I pray. Give me the peace that comes from faithful praying. At times I am so exhausted that I feel as if all foundation has given way under my feet. As if the earth has cracked and dragged me to its edge. Not even the total void of icy despair buried in the flames can separate me from your love.

For wherever I go you are by my side. If I fall you are the mother who tends my wounded bruises, if I give up you are the Father who summons courage, if I am weak at heart you are the lover who opens my soul.

Fill me as you would the ocean, I pray.

*Amen.*

## ~ *Friday* ~

Dear Father,

All I can say is thank you. Thank you for guiding me through this day with my family. I am so blessed to be surrounded by people who love me. The sun shines a little brighter this morning; the wind's chill is softened and my skin is open to your rays of hope.

Continue to walk by my side and help me in this process of maturing. Give me the patience to wait, to wait with hope to discover what you are doing in my life. Help me to accept the suffering, knowing that if I pour out the sorrow from my cup, I risk losing the joy. Bless my cup, lord, for it is mine; help me drink all of it.

*Amen.*

$\infty$ *Reflection* $\infty$

*Abba,*

*Gather me in your arms while you make an orchestra of my life. Help me to accept that this mysterious symphony has been mine since the beginning of time. Help me look up to the Divine director and pick up my violin and play.*

## ~ Saturday ~

My dear Father,

How is it possible to be fearful and yet, at the same time feel your comfort and peace? Is it possible to be in two worlds at one time, this earthly world and the world within your embrace? So many separate lives surround me, yet there is only one of you Father. You know the finite number of my heartbeats and the total sum of my breaths; you hold me and guide me through this earthly maze. Comfort me with the rhythmic waves of your heavenly sea, the soft lapping of water upon wood, the quiet call of the Shepherd's Lamb. Let me follow the soft worn prints of your Son's feet, tracked with sorrow yet lifted up in joy. *Amen.*

## ~ Sunday ~

Holy, Holy Father,

Let me bow down on bended knee before you. You know before I ask, for what I need to be forgiven. You listen before I ask, for what I need to be given.

Let me rest, Father. Let me rest at your feet. Let me feel your tender hand upon my brow.

Let me cherish this moment with all the sanctity it deserves, for this moment too, shall pass…just as the river flows to the sea…never stopping. Reassure me with the rhythm of your ever flowing love that I, as a single stone, am worth the weight of all the ocean. *Amen.*

## ~ Monday ~

O God,

I am so very near to giving up. I can't find words to pray, and I ask you to intervene, you know what I need. Take the uncertainty from my presence and protect me.
*Amen.*

## ~ Tuesday ~

Loving Father,

How can I speak my gratitude? What you have done for me is beyond my comprehension. You have answered my prayers. You have sent friends to sit with me, to pray with me, to cherish and love me. They are emissaries from you sent to intervene. In my weakness, you answered my prayer when I didn't even know what I should pray for, nor how I should pray.

Stay with me as I find stable ground and lead me often to the still waters to drink with you alone so that I may be replenished in body, mind and spirit.
*Amen.*

## ⚮ *Reflection* ⚮

He has been with me wherever I have gone. Genesis 35:3 NLT

Father,

The tendrils of fear creep round my being this morning. In this fear laden depression I am becoming more clearly aware that the anxiety of my weakened mind and body is the manifestation of the anxiety of my soul. Touch me in the deepest core of my soul; remind me that I need not look for you in the outside world of emotions, for you are waiting for me inside. Remind me with conviction that I am worthy and that I am loved. Lead me with soft whisperings to the inner sanctum of my spirit where we may sit alone together in communion.

Turn my thoughts to the warmth of the sunshine, hold me up for the wind to sweep through my mind cleansing me of all negativity. Be tender with my bruised heart, for only you can heal me. Keep me yielding and soft; create in me a new brain, shaped from the clay of my mind. Be ever present at my side. Anoint me with the oil of your preservation; teach me that although the shadow lengthens into the dark night, the dark night unfolds into the light of a new beginning. Let us be there to receive it.

*Amen.*

### ⟅ *Reflection* ⟆

*As women of courage, let us bond together and follow Christ, as a mother would her own son.*

Father God,

I am becoming so much more aware of my story with you. Help me to understand that the physical pain in my body comes from carrying years of grief and anger. Show me, when I do not know how, the way to love and accept and forgive my body for hurting. Take away my rejection of my body, the sometimes overwhelming feelings of wanting to punish my body for carrying what I don't want.

Teach me acceptance. Above all, teach me patience, how to wait in the middle of suffering for your hand. Answer my prayers when I don't even know what help to ask for. Send my love and forgiveness to those I cannot approach, through your Son, Jesus Christ. I ask him to help bear this burden for me because I do not know how to carry it.

*Amen.*

~ *Friday* ~

Healer God,

I stand before you trembling, my mind and body hurting. I ask that you salve me with the oil of your healing. I ask because I am weak, and pain is so difficult when I am depressed. Lift my spirits and renew my gratitude so that I may see colors again, feel the wind on my cheek and know the connection of which my friends speak. One after another tells the story of times that I have been there for them, and they pour out their gratitude to me.

Help me understand that I will forever carry those stories in my heart and they will awaken again. Keep me strong enough to share my gifts with others.

*Amen.*

## ~ *Saturday* ~

Abba, my Father,

Grow my faith; let it emerge from the final reluctant seed pod and grow ever upward toward the light. Shower me with rain, kiss me with sun, help me stand upright in a place of bold trust, knowing the Lord's offerings are abundant. Shelter me, protect me, trust me to love you, O Lord. In your blessed Son's name,

*Amen.*

## ~ *Sunday* ~

Abba,

Teach me how to enjoy the present Father, knowing full well that tomorrow may arrive still laden with difficulties. Shore up my hands and arms so that I am ready to carry my burden long after you have decreased its heavy weight.

Teach me how to surrender, how to find joy in the walking. Show me the way to simplicity. Turn my anxiety into Hope. Watch over me tonight as I sleep. Give me restful peace and renewal for tomorrow.

*Amen.*

## ~ Monday ~

Abba,

Help me understand that my body is a gift from you, it is not my own. You formed it, you made me one of a kind. Teach me respect for my body, for then I will learn of your promise... to watch over me and prepare me for life in the Spirit. Give me the wisest teachings to learn from. Prepare me in mind, body and spirit for the celebration of life in Jesus Christ.
*Amen.*

## ~ Tuesday ~

Father, Let me pray from my heart, not as I think others would want, but as a direct petition to you for strength. You know my every weakness; you know my fear. Help me understand that fear is not of you God, therefore it has no power over me. It is like the turbulent water of the river rapids, I need not go there.

When I am at my weakest send me a conduit upon which I may place my simple pleas for help, knowing that they come straight to you. Erase the dark borders of doubt that confine my thinking; lift my parched body from the sands of the desert which threaten to dry out my soul. Transport me to the oasis of your mercy where there is sufficient water for all who come proclaiming, "I am thirsty."

Ease my mind into the restful waters that speak of your promise of deliverance from suffering.
*Amen.*

## ~ Wednesday ~

Father,

I walk the well worn boards of my anxiety, questioning the purpose of my suffering. Is it not enough to know that you have already planned my deliverance long before the suffering began? Lift the unbearably heavy and arduous responsibility I harbor to take care of my self. Reassure me with your steady hand that I am on the right path and we are on this journey together.

Help me set aside the unnecessary and meaningless worry and stress of not knowing the particular stops and byways, the detours and unexpected stations along this journey. Rather let me focus on the final destination which will carry me to you.

Prepare my heart with courage, embolden my mind and strengthen my body. Most of all, let your spirit unfold within me so that I may be ready to accept the most beautiful mystery of all, which is you Abba.

*Amen.*

### ✖ *Reflection* ✖

My Father,

At times the fear in me rises to confront the unknown. Why be afraid I ask? Would a father allow his child to be hurt?

## ~ Thursday ~

Abba,

Use me. Help me turn my life completely over to you so that I may live the life you wrote for me before I was born, knowing that you chose my one soul for this very time and for this specific purpose. Bless me to be the story you are telling through my life.

*Amen.*


## ~ Friday ~

Blessed God,

My gratitude flows quiet like a stream through moss velvet banks. In cool shade, I sit in silence and listen to morning prayers in holy whispers. I hear melody in birdsong, joy in laughing water, communion in pregnant raw earth.

If I were to search my whole life I would not find even one place where you are not. Thank you for loving me.

*Amen.*


## ⋉ *Reflection* ⋊

*As the deer pants for streams of water, so my soul pants for you, O God.* Psalm 42:1

*~ Saturday ~*

Abba,

If ever I needed you I need you now. There is not a single word I can utter that will convey my petition to a mere mortal. Yet I need no words with you. Long ago you heard the most primitive of all sounds...the small sweet sighing of my soul before you placed me in my body.

Come to me now, touch my brow so that I may feel loved and not forgotten. You formed my prayers before I was born, you gave me your assurance in answers that have been waiting until this time. Open my heart and let my infant soul speak to me the answers from you, O God.

*Amen.*

*Reflection*

All the days ordained for me were written in your book before one of them came to be. Psalm 139:16

## ~ Sunday ~

Father,

I feel so unworthy. I would trade this soul pain for pain of another kind, yet I know that my life is not for bargaining. I don't even know how to let you work in my life. I feel like an imposter, like one who poses prayers and hides her face from you.

Use me Lord; develop my patience. This illness has weakened my mind, body and spirit. If you wish me to go on I ask you to help me. Guide me now into surrender. Let me know you have always held your arms open for me. Let there be peace with me. *Amen.*

## ~ Monday ~

Father,

What is it you want from me? I have nothing left to give except my surrender. I have exhausted all sensibilities and stand before you trembling and weak. I pray for strength to go on. Nothing seems rational any longer, my world is shrinking, I am forgetting who I am.

Please lift me up in your arms and cradle me as you would an infant daughter. Lovingly hold me until I am comforted, then tenderly release me, showing me how to release all fears and all distress.

Protect me from harm. Heal me so that I can once again engage in life. In your blessed Son's name,
*Amen.*

## ~ Tuesday ~

Abba, my protector,

Help me understand that this life on earth is but a moment in the breath of the universe, compared to the life you offer us in your kingdom. Prepare me in both mind and spirit to receive your Word; shower me with purpose, help me glean from my suffering the meaning in my existence. I earnestly pray to you Abba, please temper the fire in which I burn so that I may yet emerge. I know you want me refined, I ask only that you not give me more than I can bear. Deliver me soon.

*Amen.*

## ⟨ *Reflection* ⟩

For you have tried us, O God; you have refined us as silver is refined. Psalm 66:10 NASB

No testing has overtaken you that is not common to everyone. God is faithful, and he will not let you be tested beyond your strength, but with the testing he will also provide the way out so that you may be able to endure it. 1 Corinthians 10: 13 NRSV

## ~ Wednesday ~

Abba,

The anxiety of my soul outpaces me today. I cannot rest, I cannot still the beating of my worried heart. I beg of you to erase all fear from my mind, blot out darkness and despair; throw open the window of your mercy and make me whole. Bless the doctors who hold in their hands the tired remnants of my being, so that through them my soul can breathe.

*Amen.*

## ~ Thursday ~

Have mercy on me, O God.

Allow my worn out body to fall into your arms. Mold me with your Word, apply it as you would a poultice to my weary spirit. Give me strength in my muscles, courage in my heart and allow me to rest in your Grace. You have given me this day to live my best life; follow me lest I fall, capture my intentions with the passion of a life lived for you, O God. Be with me throughout this day and night.

*Amen.*

## ⟩⟨ Reflection ⟨⟩

... but those who hope in the Lord will renew their strength. They will soar on wings like eagles; they will run and not grow weary, they will walk and not be faint. Isaiah 40:31

O my God,

Trust me to move slowly toward you. My mind and body have fought hard for so long that my very soul is worn inside out. I trust that you will step with me over the very hurdles that have been placed there for me. Through all my weariness, all my frailty and weakness, you have been preparing for me. You gave me glory in success even before I had begun the battle. For you have always known my story; it was written with lambskin fingers before the birth of my ancestors. It was etched in silver at the first rising of the new moon; it was dyed in deep ocher before the clay had fired the earth. You knew me then…to be your child to do great things through you. Oh, that the path to you would be less painful, I cry out. And in the darkest fold of suffering I hear you say, "My child, come to me. I am here."

*Amen.*

⊂× *Reflection* ×⊃

*Abba, help me pray as one who expects answers, not as one who has no hope.*

## ~ Saturday ~

Dear Holy God,

Though the anxiety and depression at times sabotage my good intentions, I am praying fervently for your grace. Grace that will allow me to celebrate with my family of faith. Reassure me through this dark night that when morning comes, you will walk steadfastly beside me as I climb the church steps. Sit with me, flanking my sides with girded reinforcement for I shall need you. Lift my heart and mood in celebration of the joyful ride your Son made into Jerusalem. Forgive me when I cannot be fully present. You know my mind better than any doctor, so I rest assured that you will be pleased with my effort, even if I fall short of my own expectations.

*Amen.*

## ~ Palm Sunday ~

Father God,

Still my heart. Fill me with your peace. Let me draw upon your vast stillness. The morning brings so much anxiety that I often feel paralyzed. Inside the vacuum I do not know where to turn to find you. I feel as if you have left me all alone. Remind me now and every morning that you are here. I need not look for you, for you have already found me; you have promised to walk ever by my side. Build strong connections within my weakness and keep me safe. Let me praise and honor you on this holy day of Palm Sunday.

*Amen.*

*~ Monday ~*

Gracious Loving Father,

I am such a slow learner. It is a continuous daily process to learn that my life is really in your hands, that all the perfection I try to accomplish is so unnecessary, for my life is up to you. Why is that so difficult for me to understand? It is such a simple and consoling concept; there is nothing complicated about it. When I slip and fall into the trap of believing that I am in control, that is when the anxiety and fear are at their worst. Let me contemplate the mystery of your design, knowing that it is like a magnificent tapestry, woven thread by thread. It is perfect in design even though I do not yet see it finished.

Instill in me that quiet yet overpowering serenity that only you can give. Empty my mind of fearful thought, wield your rod and your staff to chase away my enemies. Leave me with the beginning bloom of quietude.

*Amen.*

∝ *Reflection* ∝

What if the last stone unturned is to leave some stones unturned? *[from a guide on my journey]*

## ~ *Tuesday* ~

Abba,

Imprint in me the precious memory of this day, so that when troubled days come again, I will call on your name and you will help me remember the goodness of this day. Today sun rays streamed gloriously through my kitchen window while I sat in reverent prayer. Lift up all those, whose names are too numerous to count, who are praying for me. Friends, known and unknown, I feel the depth of each and every prayer offered up for my good health.

Be with me tonight as I rest. Give me the dreams of a cherished child in sleep. In your precious Son's name, who bore all our suffering upon his wounded body.

*Amen.*

## ~ *Wednesday* ~

Dear Lord,

I have thrown the door wide open. I am in the watchtower waiting with expectant hope upon my breath. Settle your spirit within my soul; lead me to answers to tomorrow's prayers. Gentle my heart to receive your blessings. Brace me with strength to live the story you have set forth for my life. Give me courage to walk the stony steps of this rocky plateau. Hold me close so that I may walk upon your feet when mine are weak. I need you this much.

*Amen.*

## ~ *Thursday* ~

Abba,

There are breezes whispering through me today, unsettling, but not altogether unpleasant. Pass your hand upon the winds so that they become as mild as the stirring of the tall grass by the still lake at dusk. As I face this new day, let one teardrop of your merciful silence fall into the water so that I may feel its ever expanding circles of empathy and calm. Let the new rain of this spring wash me clean so that you may give me rebirth.

Quiet my anxious heart; let me pray without ceasing in anticipation and assurance of your promise to carry my burden. *Amen.*

## ~ *Friday* ~

Gracious Father,

Walk with me on this Good Friday as I think of the suffering of your Son. Turn my face toward the cross; place in my heart the assurance of resurrection and light.

Thank you for the miracle of walking me through each day. Continue to provide me with strength. When I feel weak and depleted, fill me to overflowing with your love, manifested in your Son, and in my church family who are praying for me.
*Amen.*

*~ Saturday ~*

Abba,

What is faith? How do I learn faith? Do I grow faith? Is it something I need to work at or is it simply an act of surrender? Is it finally coming to the point where I can stop wanting my own way and ask you, Father, to lead me in your way? Is it moving beyond the disappointment over failed desires, and asking you to take charge of my direction?

I am so tired tonight, another day of disappointments, of having things turn out other than what I expected or had hoped for. Perhaps you are still trying to get my full attention. Perhaps you are not finished pruning this branch that I am. You call me to wait patiently while you tend to the garden of my soul. It is so very painful at times, yet if you were to leave me alone, I am afraid the chaos might crowd out my true self. I would be full of the seeds of discontent and the brambles of hostility. The bloom of my spirit would be extinguished in the dark. So I say yes, Lord, tend me with such exquisite care that I might pour forth in such bright color and heady fragrance that I live a full and radiant life for you.

*Amen.*

## ~ *Sunday* ~

Halleluiah!

Easter morning is here and I feel so blessed to be alive. My church family embraced me this morning with love as deep and warm as the summer sun. I feel loved and so much a part of a faithful community of prayer. Lord, turn my face to the good, to the strong, to the positive. Let me touch and be touched by Angel wings that keep me sturdily on the right path.

*Amen.*

## ~ *Monday* ~

O Lord,

The Grace Givers in my daily life have become things of such simplicity. Being reduced to a fraction of my usual busy self, I find grace in simple acts of awareness. A quiet mind, a favorite hymn, a relaxed body. I find this time of healing to be so necessary to the development of my spiritual life; this silent almost cloistered space I've fashioned to contain my mind and spirit is full of your healing Grace.

I give thanks for your presence and for your teachings through the Bible. Continue to lead me so that I delight in following you.

*Amen.*

## ~ Tuesday ~

My Father,

I hear the song "One Day at a Time" and I am reminded that all I need do is to look no farther than today for your guiding presence, that your strength is sufficient for me today. I need not worry about tomorrow as you have given me your promise that you will be with me then as you are now.

Turn my eyes outward past the narrow focus of my own suffering to find new meaning in what I can do to further your work.

*Amen.*


## ~ Wednesday ~

Abba,

I stray from your word as the dark of doubt creeps in. It is a sad and lonely thing to doubt in my own self-worth. Stop with a sudden and authoritative hand the randomness of my negative thoughts and emotions. Invite me into the golden aura of your presence, invite me now.

Clear my mind, let it be fresh and clean, glistening like the soft velvet of a rose petal after a summer rain. Help me wait with you. You have a flawless design for me. Although it is a mystery to me now, give me a glimpse of the peace that awaits me on the other side of this turmoil.

You proclaim that if we wait with expectant hope, you shall not disappoint us. If we wait with a closed door, we shall not be ready to meet you when you come.

Examine my heart and soul, open every door, window, shutter and attic sill so that I may be ready for you. Sit with me today; teach me to wait with hope.

*Amen.*

## ~ *Thursday* ~

My dear Abba,

You have my full attention, I am at a loss as to what I need to do next. Perhaps that is precisely what you have been telling me, "Do nothing, just hold the faith quietly, yet firmly in your heart. And wait, for I have been preparing for you long before your suffering began. I knew the trials you would face; I even knew how difficult would be your struggle. I knew that your trials would be lengthy, heart rending, and soul searching, and that you would want them to end long before the time I had appointed. I cry real tears to see you suffer, to hear the plaintive cries as the fabric of your soul is torn. Be strong my child. I have sent soul-lending warriors to march with you. Do not underestimate their strength for I have fortified them with the Holy Spirit.

Open your whole being my child; let me mend the gaping wound in your soul through the work of the Holy Spirit, through prayer and through my well appointed ambassadors. I love you this much."

Abba, let me sleep the sleep of the Angels' songs; help me prepare for the miracle of life to come to my life. In your Son's name,

*Amen.*

## ~ Friday ~

Abba,

You have blessed me with strength and optimism today. My focus is on serving you. Remain by my side now and forever.

*Amen.*

## ~ Saturday ~

Father,

The gray clouds of despair circle my sky, yet if I reach I will find you. You have not disappeared; it is only I who have slipped into the crack of the stone wall. Come after me, find me and pull me back into the shepherd's fold, knowing that you rejoice over finding my one lost soul. Turn my thoughts from the pain in my body, let me use it to make me stronger. *Amen.*

## ∝ *Reflection* ∞

As a shepherd looks after his scattered flock when he is with them, so will I look after my sheep. I will rescue them from all the places where they were scattered on a day of clouds and darkness. Ezekiel 34:12

## ~ *Sunday* ~

God,

Fill me to overflowing with the grace of your salvation. Let me remember yesterday's service of the anointing with oil, oil to cleanse and purify, oil for healing of such deep internal wounds that only you God, can touch. Let me be aware of the oil of the cross on my forehead, the oil of my palms folded in prayer. Bless me, keep me, heal me.

I call upon Jesus who has all power and authority in love to lay his hands upon my illness and deliver me from its grip. I pray this in Jesus' name,
*Amen.*

## ~ *Monday* ~

Abba,

Your grace leaves me in awe that you would hear my petition for peace and answer me with a banquet set before me. I feel unworthy, yet I know that there is nothing I need do to deserve your love. All my sins have been forgiven and you have graced me with a clean slate, as new and pristine as the first morning of creation abundant with holy light.

Lead me I pray across the drought of hot desert sands, through the flood roaring down the rocky gorge, and into the rich oasis of your bountiful presence. Be with me now.
*Amen.*

Abba,

As I read the psalms I am comforted, for the very same soul hunger is evident there as I experience now. Bless my spiritual mentor who graced me today with a reading of Psalm 40: 1-3. Let my words rise to meet King David's in this mutual cry for help; let me be comforted by your presence just as so many have been before me. Forgive me my shortcomings, I want to come to you now.

I too ask for deliverance and give praise to the God who makes all possible.

I am but a noisy gull fighting for bits of sustenance, yet God hears my raucous cry, too despairing for words. He sends his Holy Spirit to help me wait patiently so that I may be like the quiet dove in the morning dawn before sunrise. The Lord lifted me out of the chaos of my internal strife, out of the driving rain and the froth stirred sea. He set my mind on a steady keel and charted my course as I navigated stormy waters. He has given me a new course to sail. Praise God; let many see the luminous light of his transpirations within my soul. I fall on my knees in amazement that he would do this for me. Many blessings will flow like the rising tide on those who trust in the Lord.

*Amen.*

## ~ Wednesday ~

O Lord,

You are day by day giving me strength and confidence in my body, mind and spirit. I felt lost as a wanderer in a deep canyon, one who could not find the path to scale the steep wall. Yet all the while as I blindly pushed forward alone trying to forge my own path, you were calling to me. My heart raced with fear, I felt my enemies, the self-doubt and the shameful lies pursuing me and so I pushed on, not pausing long enough to hear the beautiful song you made of my name. I felt lost, yet you knew I was found. I felt afraid, yet you knew I was safe. I felt alone, yet you knew I was with you. Upon surrender, I slowed my pace and let your love catch up with me. My gratitude is so very great. *Amen.*


## ~ Thursday ~

O Holy Father,

I feel so weak in faith at times…. so afraid and alone, yet I know that your arms encircle me every minute of every day. I hear your voice call to me, "Surrender my child. There is no trial too great for you to face when I am with you. I am ever at the ready to catch you when weakness overtakes you. Do not be afraid to fall, for I am here."

Lord, still my racing thoughts, let the slow quiet rhythms of your holy grace fill me from the inside out. Lead me in this grace filled dance of life to a deeper commitment to you. *Amen.*

## ~ Friday ~

Father God,

Fear is not of God; I must remember this. Though I cannot trust my mind and body at the present moment, please Father God, send the Holy Spirit to wrap me in loving arms. Reassure me that my walk is safe, that I need not be perfect, that I need only to trust in you. I beseech you, O God, to throw off this yoke of prattling fear and replace it with the mantle of your peace so that I may rejoin those on the path toward your presence.

Keep constant prayer on my lips today, place peace in my heart and secure me in your armor for protection from all enemies.

*Amen.*

## ~ Saturday ~

Abba,

You have graced me with a gentle day. I prayed to you and you listened and heard me. Let me pray without ceasing for faith. It is a continuous journey, day by day, hour by hour; this prayer is on my lips always, "Give me faith Lord, grace me with the blessed assurance of you in my life."

Help me accept that the journey you have planned for me in this lifetime has been chosen especially for me for a greater purpose.

You have taken me places I would not have dared to venture without you by my side. Because you, O God, know no fear, guide me to that same place where fear is not, where love is the true victor, and you are pure love.

*Amen.*

## ~ *Sunday* ~

Grace slips in like new shoots in spring, rooting firmly, gaining strength in the light and warm. With God's care, grace takes hold in my life and I am like the new spring shoot, drinking deep of the still water and singing to the sky.

When I cannot pray, I turn my face to God and wait. When I can pray, He recognizes the words born in the silence of the wait and gives me thanks for holding fast to His name.

If this is a time of deep sorrow for you, dear reader, and you have no words for prayers upon your lips, take comfort in knowing that all my prayers were born of the Holy Spirit just for you and for me. May God hold us all close while we walk through the shadows; let him deliver us up into the brilliance of his presence.

*Amen.*

## ∝ *Reflection* ∞

*I wait for the Lord, my soul waits, and in his word I put my hope.* Psalm 130:5

*I am afraid, still my heart. I am alone, fill me with you.*

O Gracious God,

I am so blessed to have so many people praying for me; you have heard their prayers on my behalf and have intervened with mercy and love. The day has passed with gratitude upon my lips; every minute I have been thanking you. The darkness is entering the dawn, the heaviness has lightened, and the sealed door has been thrown open by your mighty command. I stand in utter awe that you would reach down to me and lift me from the chaos of fear.

You have set my mind in order according to your divine plan, you have touched every cell in my body with your mercy. It has been so long since I have known such peace.

Help me live this day resting in your arms, patiently waiting with expectant hope for healing. In my suffering, my groaning has been transformed to praise, my tears to joy, my prayers for release to thanksgiving.

Forgive me Father for the times I have lived in the dark of doubt, for those unbearable moments when I felt I could wait no longer. Lay your gentle hand upon my head and acknowledge the frailty of my humanity, for you know that I have done the best that I can.

*Amen.*

*~ Tuesday ~*

Abba,

When I feel weakest in faith give me courage to keep believing. Stand me up, fill me with your grace and propel me toward the person you believe I am. If Jesus were here today I would show no hesitation in fitting my hand to his hand, my steps to his steps, knowing that I would never measure up. Yet I know that because he took the fall for me, all he wants is my willing heart. Abba, keep me willing, keep me walking on this journey to you.

*Amen.*

⚮ *Reflection* ⚮

*How precious to me are your thoughts, O God! How vast is the sum of them! Were I to count them, they would outnumber the grains of sand. When I awake, I am still with you.* Psalm 139:17-18

## ~ Wednesday ~

Abba,

Hold me tenderly, let me rest a blessed peace in your arms. I am so very tired. I cannot walk any more tonight so I ask you to carry me. My surrender comes to you unveiled and undisguised. I am so exhausted; I know so well that none of my efforts at holding myself together are in my control. It is all in your hands. I hear Jesus call my name and ask, "My child, do you want to be healed?" I reach out to touch the hem of his garment, for "Yes, I do want to be healed." Let me have as much faith as the woman on the road beside Jesus, for then, I too may hear, *Take heart, daughter; your faith has made you well.* Matthew 9: 22
*Amen.*

## ~ Thursday ~

Abba,

Exhaustion overwhelms me. There are days of wanting to give up, of wanting to say, "There is a young mother, a young child somewhere, take me instead, let them live." But you call me back and remind me yet once again, that my life is not mine to give or take. It is yours Abba, it is all yours. Let me be thankful for all the things I am blessed with: home, family, companionship. Take my discouragement, my fatigue, my resignation and hold them for me today so that I may rest. Fill me with your love and peace so that I may live in deeper faith with you.
*Amen.*

## ~ Friday ~

Abba,

Let me walk your mountain tops, let me sing into the wide open spaces, let praise blossom on my lips like the wild lupine in spring. Let me climb higher than ever before, upon the snow capped peaks; let my trust soar like the eagles on the updrafts to heaven.

*Amen.*

## ~ Saturday ~

Father,

Take all discouragement and fear from me O, Lord. I do not know what more you want of me Lord; let me be patient until you reveal your plan for me. I have so little energy today; help me sleep in blessed peace tonight. Jesus, take my hand within your folded praying hands; hold me close to your heart, let me feel the beating of your heart within me. Hold onto me, never let me go. Love me completely, I pray.

*Amen.*

## ✂ *Reflection* ✂

*There is no fear in love; but perfect love casts out fear ...*
1 John 4:18 NASB

Lord,

I lift your name on high. Teach me to walk slowly with my face always turned to you so that I may see the simple way in which you lead me in all things. Fill my mouth with words of celebration. In the slow small dark hours of the night, give me the words to sing softly of your love. In the midst of the world's noise, show me how to listen for the recapitulation of your merciful refrain. Impress upon me that I need never fear that you will leave me alone to sing solo…it always has been and always will be a duet between the lover and the loved. Gather me up in your arms when I lose the melody, whisper in my ear when I forget the words, direct the orchestra of Angels who surround me, ever at the ready to lead me in the greatest symphony of all time. A love story larger than any earthly drama, a love story born on the eve of creation, a love story where you profess the magnitude of your unconditional love for me.

Yes, for me, you have wiped clean and forgiven all my sins so that you can love me that much more. Help me lay down the scores of my pretenses, the instruments of mere mortals, the baton of self-power; direct me to bow down on my knees to be escorted into your heavenly symphony. Show me my place, let me know it has been mine forever and that without my melody, your orchestra is not complete. Invite all your children to join this celestial concert now.
*Amen.*

## - *Monday* -

Father,

I am waiting and I am weak. Hold me up while you wait with me. I don't know how to do this, even while you hold my hand I am trembling. I feel so unprotected today, even though I know you still walk with me. I ask you to take my hand and hold me tighter than ever before and I will hold as tightly as I possibly can.

Place your armor on me to protect me, for I cannot see and I don't know the way. Just hold me, even carry me until I am strong enough to put my feet back on the ground. Help me walk with you out of this darkness and into the light. Still my panic and be a presence with me today.

Thank you for choosing me to be your child.

*Amen.*

⤙ *Reflection* ⤚

For what I do not know, teach me.

## ~ Tuesday ~

Abba,

I am beginning to understand how vast your love is, and how grateful I am that you chose to love me as your child. Trusting you without reservation has been a difficult thing for me, but I am learning that you love me unconditionally. You have formed a plan for me that will bring me to you. Help me Heavenly Father, help me surrender all.
*Amen.*

## ~ Wednesday ~

Abba,

I need courage today to face the ordinary tasks of my daily life. I feel caught between the world of hope and the world of despair. I am sighing the sighs that only you can hear, that only you can fashion into a prayer for guidance. You have followed me when I am running, you have walked beside me when my pace has faltered, you have lain down beside me when I have collapsed with exhaustion. I ask you now to place your hand of healing upon my broken heart, my broken mind and my broken body. I ask you for a day that unfolds with hope, like the eagle that soars on the updrafts of optimism. I ask you for a day that is gentle and kind, a day that I can trust.
*Amen.*

Father God,

Do I believe in miracles? Surely I do, for you have graced me with a miracle tonight. You have taken anxiety and fear from me; you have blessed me with a heart entrained to the rhythmic beating of Angel wings. You have slowed my racing thoughts, and have replaced them with the slow rolling surf of thanksgiving prayers. My eyes see a new horizon, my ears hear a new earth song, my fingers are blessed to touch new skin where the old has fallen away.

In the long dark cave of despair, there seems no end to the dark, no glimmer of light… whether day or night. But you come into my presence; you throw the flame of salvation to light a thousand candles surrounding me. So bright is it I can barely look upon it. There is no mistake, you have called me to wait and I am waiting, through hardship and suffering, through doubt and despair. At times I wait poorly, convinced I am an insignificant bit of humanity. Yet you have come to tell me otherwise.

There is no mistake, you have come for me.

*Amen.*

## ⤢ *Reflection* ⤣

*Praise God, who did not ignore my prayer or withdraw his unfailing love from me.* Psalm 66:20 NLT

## ~ *Friday* ~

Abba,

Thank you for my friend who prayed with me, who stayed with me, through dark and lonely moments. Lift her up as an Angel of mercy, a befriender of the lonely.

Give me energy today to turn my sorrow into a prayer of thanksgiving, a prayer thanking you for my very life.

Turn my thoughts from those dark caves of despair. Turn my face toward the light. Sit with me in lonely corners, walk with me in noisy faceless streets, hold me on the darkest ledges of the night; through all this let me praise your name and thank you for choosing me to be your child. Thank you for sending sweet Jesus to us so that we could know that your love is without bounds, that your love is endless. Give me hope to go on living.

*Amen.*

### ∝ *Reflection* ∝

*He will cover you with his feathers, and under his wings you will find refuge; his faithfulness will be your shield and rampart.* Psalm 91:4

Father of all Love,

Shower me with the precious petals of your forgiveness, the radiant blossoms of your gracious love; show me the charity and compassion of this world that I never imagined possible. Hold me as one who is a dear child, orphaned by this limited earthly kingdom, yet to be a part of your heavenly family. Let me drink in the sweet tenderness of your caring, let me stand in awe of the beauty of your art, let me open my heart and say, "Sweet Lord, come in, come in. Cleanse me from the inside out. Throw out all tormenters from the being of my vessel, fill me from the inside out with all the goodness that emanates from you. Bless me now."

*Amen.*

✂ *Reflection* ✂

*I will not leave you as orphans; I will come to you.* John 14:18

Almighty Lord,

*This is the day which the Lord has made; let us rejoice and be glad in it.* Psalm 118: 24 NASB

I give you thanks for the wind sighing through the pine wood forest; I give you thanks for the soft purple veil on the snow mountains at sunset. I give you thanks for the quiet coming and going of the fishermen's tide, for the ebb and flow of the water that sustains us when our lips are parched and we are unable to pray. Lord there is so much in this world to give thanks for. For all things are from you and in you.

I look upon the mystery of the changing seasons within my heart and know that there is purpose in the searing heat of summer, in the bone-chilling cold of winter. I know that you have sculpted my purpose in the seascapes of the ocean swells, you have written it on the dunes of the desert, you have celebrated it in the farthest flung stars of the universe. There is no mistake in my being born a child of God. Help me when I turn away from your glorious call; open my ears to hear you proclaiming that I am exactly as you have made me, and you love me just as I am.

Give me the strength to look each day at my reflection in Jesus' face and know that I will fall short; I will fall short and ask forgiveness and I will try again. That is all that Jesus wants, that we give our best at the moment when we are weakest; perhaps that may simply be a plaintive cry for help.

He hears our cry and he understands the pain, the sorrow, the suffering of life on this earth. He died to give us hope; hope that we can rise above all earthly pain with his help, and that we are on our way to a more beautiful life in his presence.

Lord, I give you all glory and honor.

*Amen.*

## ~ Monday ~

Abba,

Guide me when I write to you so that the writing is more than a prayer without genuine listening; let me truly commit to my prayers, let me live them, word by word, earnestly and authentically. Let my prayers be more than simple prayer flags fluttering in the breeze sent to the heavens on questioning hope. Continue to teach me a prayerful attitude, one of expectant hope, of the assurance of a kind and merciful loving God who touches me with answers to my prayers in his time... in his time. I believe he hears me; I commit to his answer and I will live fully into the life he has lovingly planned for me.

*Amen.*

## ~ Tuesday ~

Abba,

You have opened my eyes to a new day. I cried out to you and you turned to me with arms as wide as the newborn sky, with love as deep as the sea, with a heart as big as the infinite universe. You scooped me up before my cry was on my lips, you enfolded me in robes washed sparkling white, you fed me manna from your own table. You came to me in the place where the cup of sorrow meets the cup of joy, for you knew I was drowning. You tenderly lifted me out of the lake of sorrows, you placed me on the fertile bank where tall grasses whisper the psalms of the scripture. You laid my head on a mat woven of absolute truth and I knew without a doubt that you had come just for me, that you had come to save me.

*Amen.*

### ⊂× *Reflection* ×⊃

*Thank you Abba for such relief of pain and suffering. My gratitude swells like the sea submitting to the moon. It all has purpose, every moment, whether in pain or in joy. My cup has never been fuller; I have never been nearer to drinking all of it. Keep me close.*

My Protector God,

Though my heart wants to sing praises, my mind and body still tremble with the fear of separation from you, O Lord. Today I ask that you still my obsessive thinking, quiet my ruminations, and pass your hand gently through the valleys of my brain, bringing your peace to the random floods of disharmony. Connect the pathways that have been overgrown with random brambles, thorns and briars. Landscape my mind with the rose of resurrection, the mimosa of mercy and the lavender of your love.

Instill in me this prayer, "Lord Jesus Christ, I believe that fear is not of God, therefore it has no authority or power over me. I believe that you have all power and authority to cast out all evil thoughts, temptations and spirits, those which seep with such subtlety into my mind I do not hear their coming. Fill me with your love so there is no room for the other. Grace me with your healing and the sweet sense of your peace."

Lord, let this become the prayer that is ever on my lips today. Stay close to me throughout the long hours of this day, surround me with your perfect protection. Carry me softly into the indigo of night, wrap me in the warm mantle of your arms while the soft moonlight of your grace illuminates my soul.

*Amen.*

Abba, Abba,

The fire is so hot, how long do you want me here? There are times I feel I am being punished, but I do not believe that a loving Father would hurt an already suffering child. I have to believe that you are sparing me anguish even more intense than what I now endure. Without that belief, without trust and faith in you God, none of this has meaning. If you want me to do your work I need some reassurance that you are going to deliver me from this agonizing state of mind. I have to believe that you will, because I have no where else to turn. I am empty, I am on my knees, I surrender, what more is it you want of me? I know that I am responding as a woman who is utterly alone and desperate. "Where is your faith my child?" you ask. "You are never alone, never."

I know that no human, neither man nor woman, can step into this internal inferno and hold me. Only your Son Jesus can do this for me. Is it that you think I have not enough faith yet? Is there something I am to wait for, something more that I am to find polished and refined from the fire?

I am frail God, and I am scared. You know my breaking point, you know that each time I believe I have reached it, you push me to dig deeper within my soul and take another step toward you. How many times have I cried out for you, Abba, and each time you have been there?

Although I do not feel your presence, nor hear you, nor see you, your Word assures me that you are here. You are here by my side.

Perhaps if I were to see you, the sorrowful lines across your face would be too unbearable to witness. Perhaps that is why we must believe without seeing…because you are carrying the weight of the world's sorrows etched on your loving face, and I would instantly recognize the deep chasm of pain that you bear for me.

*Amen.*

### ~ Friday ~

Abba,

I need a miracle tonight. I ask because I believe everything is possible in you. Thank you, Abba, for choosing me to be your child. Save my life, I pray, save my life.

*Amen.*

### ✂ *Reflection* ✂

*Put on all of God's armor so that you will be able to stand firm against all strategies of the devil.* Ephesians 6:11 NLT

My Abba, Abba, Abba,

How can I give thanks enough for what you have done for me. You have graced me with the most blessed and peaceful day that I have had in months. There is nothing but peace and harmony flowing through the veins of my worn out, but rejoicing body. You have said you would carry me and you have. Again I ask you to remove all fear and doubt from my being; let me hold this day fast in my mind as a constant reminder that you hear my cry for help and you reach down to touch me with loving grace.

In days to come, when the tendrils of self-doubt come trickling through the folds of my mind, take me firmly by the hand and turn my steps toward all that is beautiful and positive.

Imprint in my soul the image of your Son Jesus, holding my hand fast in his. Guide me to ever hold tight to his hand, for it is I, not he, who weakens the clasp of my hand in his.

Guide me to take each day slowly, savoring all, knowing that healing happens under your watchful eye. All I need do is rest in your promise.

*Amen.*

## ∝ *Reflection* ✕⊃

*He has made everything beautiful in its time. He has also set eternity in the hearts of men; yet they cannot fathom what God has done from beginning to end.* Ecclesiastes 3:11

## ~ Sunday ~

Abba,

Be with me today as I continue my journey of faith and self-reflection. Bestow gentleness upon my therapist and me as our session unfolds, for you know that I am doing the best that I can as I travel this most painful and difficult journey with you. Help us to remember that although we both want healing and recovery for me, it is with greater purpose and mystery that you lead us together toward the light. Be easy with my soul today, give me the breath that sighs upon the wind and the cradling that sways among the trees.

Deliver me from the tempest of this storm, I pray.

A day of rest, let me praise your name.

*Amen.*

## ~ Monday ~

Glorious Father,

At times I feel I understand nothing about this earthly life and my purpose. I feel I am part of a mystery and because of that I feel afraid at times. I search for trust, which has been for many years, foreign to me. Help me to celebrate now, so that trust becomes my friend, and reliance on God follows as easily as the blooming of forget-me-nots in the stream of fertility.

When the flame burns brightest in my soul, give me peace and assurance that I will not be burned, but instead, I will be purified for a life in God.

Continues >

Help me to claim the flame, the passion, and the faith of Jesus Christ so that my aloneness may melt into living water, and I will become, not separate, but part of the ocean that surrounds and sustains us all.

*Amen.*

## ~ Tuesday ~

Father God,

I thank you for the friends in my life who have scooped up my brokenness and held it like rose petals on a silver tray. I know that you have sent these Angels to help me walk through the dark shadows of these days and I give you thanks. They have sat with me through anxious darkening skies, through storms of tears, through howling winds, and they have not once turned to run away. How much more steady and precious than that, must be your constant presence with me, through all darkness and despair.

When I feel most alone, I seek you out, knowing I have no further to go than to turn inward to the inner chamber of my heart, to the inner sanctum of my soul. For you have promised me that you wait for me there. How can I ever feel I am alone when I know that even as you are in me, you also carry me. You carry me like water to the very well of my existence, and you drink from the well in communion with me. Yes, you drink in communion with me.

*Amen.*

## ~ Wednesday ~

O my Father,

Despair circles me tonight like fog through which I cannot see. Although I know despair, I will not turn away. And neither, will I give in. I will hold fast to your hand and ask you more fervently for protection. Place my feet, one by one, upon the path to you. Although it is rocky now, assure me that in your time it will be transformed into a walk in the garden meadow of your kingdom. A meadow full of sky in azure blue, flowers in fuchsia pink, and radiance in golden yellow. A garden with the essence of anointing oils, the fragrance of the heavenly bouquet upon the banquet table, the illumination of dew drops shining like bejeweled crowns.

While we struggle with the imperfection in this world, in the midst of such heavenly perfection you call to us, you call us as your children to share with you the feast that awaits us in your Son Jesus Christ. The feast that never runs dry, the feast that never turns us away, the feast that will nourish us forever more.

*Amen.*

### ✐ *Reflection* ✐

*Abba, lead me to your table where salvation is abundant.*

## ~ Thursday ~

Abba, Abba,

I am scared, I am alone, and I am a child. These thoughts and others reverberate through my mind like clanging keys on the metal bars where Paul was imprisoned. Oh, but that you would give me just one ounce of his courage, his strength, his faith. I feel so inadequate, so poor in faith. The pain in my body weakens my resolve, yet I know you will touch it with your healing hand and pronounce me fit to serve. When the doubt comes raging out of the shadow, turn my face to you, with my back on the doubt; fit my feet with wings so that I may outrun all darkness and despair in my flight to you.

Grace me with your holy presence as I sit in solemn silence and petition you for help. Let me know with all of my heart that your delay is not denial. Place upon me the patience of Job so that I may wait for your deliverance.

Turn my suffering into a prayer that echoes across time and space and speaks for all who suffer tonight.

Abba, let my breath of inspiration be heard as a soft sigh round the world as I call for your help.

Help all of us who suffer; lessen the pain, the physical, the mental, the emotional and the spiritual. Make our lives whole so that we may do your work.

In your blessed Son's name,
*Amen.*

O Holy God,

There is nothing left in this shell of a person where I used to live. I cry out in anguish for your deliverance and I feel abandoned. I understand that my illness is a gift from you so that I will turn to you and surrender completely. It is indeed a mystery why you want me to go through such pain; I just know that I must hang on more tightly to your hand for you have never let me go. I feel my heart breaking with each passing moment and I wonder if your tears are for me or for the broken world. There is so much suffering on this earth, and yet you want us to rejoice in the joy of the moment.

Perhaps that is all I can expect during this intensity, that I see the wild blue iris and I turn to you with gratitude. Take my heart, take my mind, take my spirit, take all of me and hold me in your hand so that I may mold my shape into your God filled palm, and that you may fill my God shaped emptiness with your love.

*Amen.*

## ✂ *Reflection* ✂

*But, as for me, I am like a green olive tree in the house of God; I trust in the loving kindness of God forever and ever.* Psalm 52:8 NASB

## ~ Wednesday ~

Abba,

I have been away from praying for several days and I feel the dry wind blowing in the wilderness. I am reaching for you even now as I feel the hot sand driving through my fingertips. I feel your hand near me; may I grasp it and hold tightly until the arid plain passes into the new green spring that rises from your ever present well. Help me kneel before you, bless me with the grace of your forgiveness for all my shortcomings.

Teach me Father, the lessons of forgiveness, knowing that I am an infant in this endeavor. Lead me one step at a time as we climb together the stairs that have overgrown with the weeds, thorns and barbs I have scattered over the years. Help me strive not for perfection in this lesson, but for honesty, integrity, and completeness. Accompany me as I begin on this journey of faith and forgiveness that for years you have been inviting me to embark upon.

Bit by bit, help me remove the stones of hurt, resentment, anger and isolation from the living fabric of my beating heart. Teach me that a heart full of stones is too heavy to soar on the wings of love. Teach me that a heart full of stones invites the master spirit of rejection to take up residence…a residence so parched and bare that living love will be pushed to the far corners of the four chambers and forgotten. Hold my tongue still when angry words want to fly from my mouth.

Help me to forgive and accept the imperfections of others, knowing that my imperfections have already been forgiven by you, Lord.

Hold me in your arms and whisper in my ear that you are my Loving Father, that you will never leave me, and your love is ever present and unconditional. Tell me that you understand why the ancient anxious prints of my footsteps have been searching for the perfect mother and father on this earthly planet; that you know I have been searching for the One to hold me, longing to feel safe in arms holding tight, while listening to whispers of love stories. Love stories that tell me I am a most precious and important daughter of the universe; that there is no other like me, nor will there ever be. Show me that I may stop my searching and fall into rest in your arms. And in this stillness, feed me the seeds of forgiveness so that I may grow them in the fertile soil of my soul, so that I may bring them to maturity, all the while reaping the benefits as I bestow the fruits of forgiveness on others. For they, every one, have done the best that they could. I am not called by you to be their judge; I am called by you to grace them with my forgiveness, even in times of sharp hurts, hollow sorrow, and deep disappointment, knowing that only you Father God and your Son Jesus are perfect in Love.

Teach me that the stairway may be long and sometimes steep and slippery, and that even though I will want to turn

Continues >

around to climb down, you expect me to stay close by your side as I learn and practice this special gift of yours called forgiveness.

Father, I imagine that this lesson is not easily learned and will not be a revelation or a one time experience. I know that I will stumble and fall down, but that you will grace me with the dignity to resume my climb toward the peace and freedom that are born of forgiveness. Abba, help me commit to this journey. Stay close by my side and encourage me along the way.
*Amen.*

### ~ *Thursday* ~

Abba,

Words of prayer and praise have been on my lips throughout each day. This has been a quiet time of resting in your arms, a time of opening my senses so that I may hear even the softest rustlings of your presence. A time of allowing the gift of forgiveness to develop and grow in me. Continue to teach me how to wait with peaceful patience knowing that the answers to my prayers are already complete in heaven. From this dark underside of the storm clouds help me to envision the view you have looking down on me, Abba, through the radiant light of your source. Pour forth the prisms of light that transform my walk into a rainbow of hope.

Step into the space of my solitude, into the silent sacristy of communion; fill me in the deepest well of my being with the mother of your love and the daughter of your grace.

I praise your name and lift up my gratitude to you.
*Amen.*

## ~ Friday ~

Father,

Normal days slip by without the anxiety camped at the base of my heart, yet I feel empty when not praying from the depth of my being. My prayers cry out the loudest when I am caught in despair so dark I see no light. Yet it is now, as the light starts to filter into my mind, that I ought to pray most earnestly. In a posture of gratitude, my nakedness bathed in a lake of tears, I bow in reverence praying:

"Abba, You have answered my prayers while I have waited, even though I have waited impatiently and poorly at times. Teach me that you will reveal answers yet even greater as I learn more patience and humility. Lay your hand on me, infusing life into my already beating heart. Let me look at your creation through the eyes of a child who has been rescued from the pit of miry clay. Let me marvel at the strong hard path on which you have set my feet. Let me bear witness to those who are willing to sit with me. Help me to continue my prayers, my daily walks and conversations with you, for without you I am lost. For without you, I am nothing."

*Amen.*

## ~ Saturday ~

Abba,

Praise this day of slowly breaking dawn, of noon time sun and skies of robin egg blue. I give thanks for a quiet mind as I sit at breakfast with delicate rearrangements. I praise your name for giving me the will to live. Help me now as I embrace the overwhelming fatigue that is the aftermath of each storm. Let me lift my face to the heavens knowing that you offer me the same strong, yet tender, embrace as you did in the middle of the chaos. Scoop me up with a cheerful song and rock me lovingly in the cradle of the Angels. Give me sufficient rest and strength and a stalwart memory of the valley from which I have emerged, so that gratitude, faith and forgiveness are part of my everyday prayers. I pray all this in the name of your Son who taught us the prayers that sustain us until our final day on this earth.

*Amen.*


## ~ Monday ~

My Sweet Abba,

As my soul waits in the desert for your deliverance, let this be my prayer for today. Let me not only say the words, but also live their truths with the help of your Son Jesus Christ.

These things I pray:

I surrender. I surrender all worry, all anxiety, and all guilt. I take my hand away from the rudder of control, and surrender all to you, knowing you are preparing me for something both mysterious and sweet.

I believe. I believe you have a plan for my healing, that you have had this plan long before my suffering began.

I wait. I wait patiently in the wilderness, knowing that Jesus has already waited in the anguish of deprivation and emptiness, and that he has done this for me. Help me to feel his presence during these 40 days and 40 nights and to know that He will be at my side, holding me close, assuring me of deliverance.

I pray that you keep me mindful to the present moment and that I do all things in love, because you first loved me.

Forgive me when I fall short, acknowledge my imperfections as a human child of your love and give me your holy encouragement along the way.

I believe that you are never far from the center of my being; that upon hearing my muted cry for help, you are, in an instant ready to do battle for me against any and all forces that keep me from you.

Continue to teach me the meaning of surrender, faith, patience, love and forgiveness. Instill in me the spirit of your being, so that I am prepared to call upon you for help. *Amen.*

Holy Father,

With each seed I plant in my summertime garden, I give thanks for the living power enfolded within such a tiny wonder-at times no bigger than the eye of the smallest needle. And yet…. and yet with constant nurturing this sleeping life awakens, fed by the rain of your clouds, warmed by the light of your sun and nourished by the love infused into each embryonic seed by the plant of the parent.

You cause seeds to break open into glorious colors of bright reds, oranges, yellow, purples and pinks. There is no shade for which you are incapable of painting with your heavenly palette.

Watching each seedling emerge from the earth I am awestruck by how much heavenly design each seed carries, for the flower is perfect in every way. And in these moments, I too, feel nurtured. How much more you must care for me that you nurture me with water from your holy vessel, you feed me with the wisdom of the prophets and you warm me with the soft whisperings of your breath. Whisperings, which become the fire and the passion within my soul.

How can I despair when all is so right in my world? How can I throw my intention into the bleak darkness of the shadow of the greatest lie of all time? Give me the truth to make me bold. You have made me. I am yours. I am no mistake. Instill in me the courage to stand and face all the untruths.

Help me call on the name and the strength of your Son to extinguish such lies as quickly and simply as one does the candle left burning in the wilderness.

*Amen.*

~ *Wednesday* ~

Dear Father,

I feel as if I have lost our soulful connection. I know that you are still here by my side even though I can not feel you or see you. This is one of the times I must take a leap of faith. There are earthly distractions and personal imperfections that beg for my attention, yet I know that these take me away from you. Let me sit wrapped in your presence, though I feel empty; let me sit still, held in your arms, though I feel deserted. Show me that the wrappings that I long to discard, to tear off my body and mind are gifts from you. Inside these wrappings of anguish and suffering are true treasures that you have hidden within my heart. Were it not for the outside wrappings I would never have known there were gifts waiting inside for me.

Although my soul cries out for relief, I still turn to you God and pray, "Not my will, but thine." Come inside my body and mind, help me navigate this maze of untruths, so that I finally burst forth into the light which comes only from your truth.

Be with me tonight as I sleep. Let my mind rest and be renewed for the new day with you tomorrow.

*Amen.*

## ~ Thursday ~

Abba,

Feed me, not with the physical plants of this world, but with the musical strains of your eternal blessings. When I feel small, fill me to overflowing so that I know the largeness of your benevolence. When I feel alone come to me, in the strong fragrance of the rose petal in the wee hours of morning's dark, in the softness of newborn chicks still wet from the breaking of the shell, in the stillness of the unbroken beating of my heart. With your hands, harvest my pain and suffering so that they bear the immeasurable fruit of your generous nature. Still my impatience so that I am able to wait for the appointed time of your harvest, knowing that the long winter of hibernation is necessary for gathering energy for the prolific gifts of your spirit. *Amen.*

## ~ Friday ~

Abba,

In the light of this dusky room, sit with me in peaceful wonderment of all that has transpired in the life of the universe to converge on this perfect moment when you comfort me. Etch within my soul the mirror that reflects all that is good and brilliant in my life. Let me gather gratitude to my chest like lost lambs in blinding rain, let me offer up my gratefulness freely in the containment of your love. *Amen.*

*~ Saturday ~*

Abba,

Teach me Lord how to fight this depression, but leave the battle to you. Teach me how to surrender but not give in to despair. Plant my feet firmly in the presence of the salt of the earth so that I give you the opportunity to make my weakness my strength, *for my strength is made perfect in weakness.* [2 Corinthians 12 KJV] I know, my dear God, that you have a better life for me at the forefront of your plan and that I need only wait with expectant hope for the time you have appointed for my deliverance.

Help me become a better person because of this illness. Let me reach out in compassion to all those who suffer within the perimeters of their minds, sometimes in invisible silence. If it is your will give me the strength and the hope to walk on the smooth sanded wood of your bridges, over the silent canyons of midnight tears, so that I may say to them as you have said to me, "My child, you are never alone. You are loved. Hold on with steadfast patience and the Lord of Heaven and earth will set you free."

*Amen.*

∝ *Reflection* ∞

*Neither height nor depth, nor anything else in all creation, will be able to separate us from the love of God that is in Christ Jesus our Lord.* Romans 8:39

## ~ Sunday ~

O my God,

I feel as if my heart is breaking and I do not know where or how to find solace. Come to me, not as the subtle dusk at eventide, but boldly as the sun at the break of dawn. Show me where to walk and how to pray, *for we do not know how to pray as we should, but the Spirit Himself intercedes for us with groanings too deep for words.* Romans 8:26 NASB
*Amen.*

## ~ Monday ~

O my Lord,

I give you thanks for the peace in my soul this morning, I feel safe in the harbor of your dominion, my anchor holding fast in the tread of your feet. Yesterday's tempest is of no concern to me today, for worry and anxiety will not diminish the storm nor erase it from my memory. Teach me to let old worries drop into the sea of your omnipotent waters. When rough seas cast me into the troughs, help me to understand that I will sink under the weight of ancient anxiety and future fears. Show me that this ship we are on is too great for me to pilot, the anchor too heavy for me to carry. I have but one choice…to turn to you, palms wide open with prayer on my lips, "Abba, take the wheel; take my life and pilot me through the harbor buoys so that my journey into the open ocean will carry only the assurance of your companionship and authority to see me safely to the port you have chosen for me."
*Amen.*

## ~ Tuesday ~

My Father God,

I write from my heart this morning in both pain and joy. To know such misery is inflicted upon the world's suffering people causes me pain. To know that you have a master plan, though it be kept within the binding of your precious manuscript gives me joy…because it is only through believing this truth that I have hope that this world, my world, the world at large will survive and continue to flourish. And so I say as you have said, *Blessed are the peacemakers, for they will be called children of God.* Matthew 5: 9 My prayer is that through them our world may be saved.

Continue to light my path and lead me forward directing the story of my life as it unfolds before me. Let me live so that I reflect your teachings. Continue to teach me how to surrender, how to grow my faith, and how to let forgiveness weave itself into the fabric of my daily life.
*Amen.*

### ⊲ *Reflection* ⊳

*See how the farmer waits for the land to yield its valuable crop and how patient he is for the autumn and spring rains.* James 5:7

*Abba, help me wait with patient perseverance while I do those things that are within my power to do.*

## ~ Wednesday ~

Lord Father God,

You have said that we should ask for great things and that we can be assured we will receive them if we ask in faith. I ask you as my creator to restore my health, knowing you have the power to do this for me. Give me the courage to sit, to stand and to walk in patience as I wait for your answer, asking that your will, not mine be done. Love me, make me well, and give me the courage to persevere.

*Amen.*

## ~ Thursday ~

Abba,

Lift my eyes to the deep blue overhead and let me rest in your blessed peace. I pray from the innermost part of my heart that you teach me how to believe that you already are at work on my complete and total healing. Let me not say, "I am hoping, I am looking, I am waiting for faith to find me." Place these words solidly on my lips, "Father God, I pray that you heal me. I believe that I have received your healing this very moment for you are the God in the everlasting Now. I know I must turn to you. I believe that you have written the most beautiful song in the world for me and you have placed this song in your heart, where I may listen to it over and over each time I come to you with an honest prayer of faith."

Dear Jesus, you believed your Father so completely that prayerful night in the Garden of Gethsemane, that even though you knew the pain and suffering that would accompany the outcome you still answered, "Yes Lord." Stand by me as I take up my cross and join you in saying, "I do believe. I do believe you are healing me now."

*Amen.*

## ~ *Friday* ~

Dearest God,

I am waiting for that point when you deliver me saying, "Well done child, you were tested and you persevered. You were weak and yet you found strength; you prayed prayers more powerful than you ever thought possible. You were afraid and yet your desire for deliverance was great indeed. I always knew you would hold fast. You are like the ship built with great care and exquisite craftsmanship, for I built you myself. I have seen you through major storms; your hull has been battered by crashing waves, your deck flooded by torrential rains, your sails lagging and your keel laid nearly flat. Yet through all those long weeks and months and years of storms, the soul body of your ship did not break, though it groaned heavily and pleaded for a port in the storm. Many times you dropped anchor only to find it dragging behind you in the roiling seas.

You cried out for safe harbor and I led you through the dark and moonless night to the place where you could anchor in the solid floor of the quiet lagoon. In you I have invested much love and protection. Never be afraid to call on me; if you find yourself afraid simply look up and say, *When I am afraid I put my trust in you.* [Psalm 56: 3 ] In you child, I am pleased, for your faith will make you well."

O God, continue to walk with me, call on me to be strong, but also offer me your arms in which to rest when I can go no further. For every storm breaks into quiet waters. Abba, I need you now.
*Amen.*

## ~ Saturday ~

Abba,

Help me remember that this earthly life is so very short, but that it is the opportunity for displays of great courage and faith. Keep prayers on my lips throughout the day and let me call on your name to prevail over the master of all lies and doubt and fear. Strike him down in front of me, so I can no longer see his face, for I know that his presence haunts me at every turn. Tell me firmly and authoritatively that when I call upon my faith you are there to armor me and protect me so that I need never retreat. Keep me always on the forward path to you, even if it is one slow step at a time. *Amen.*

## ~ *Sunday* ~

Abba,

I cry out in gratitude with prayers of thankfulness for the peace you have given me today. Tears fall from my eyes, not because of sadness or sorrow, but tears of joy for you have gifted me with the miracle of respite from the depression for today. Help me to remember that there is no reason why I should not ask for great things. Today I asked for a miracle and you gave it to me. Thank you.
*Amen.*

## ∝ *Reflection* ∝

*Everything is possible for him who believes…. I do believe; help me overcome my unbelief!* Mark 9:23-24

*And the peace of God, which transcends all understanding, will guard your hearts and your minds in Christ Jesus.* Philippians 4:7

## ~ Monday ~

Thank you God,

Gratitude fills my soul like water in your abundant well, like grains of sand in the ocean floor, like the deep blue of evening twilight and the purple rose of dawn. For this day I give you thanks from the core of my being, from the place deep within my heart where my blood becomes my life source. Please bless me with more of these quiet days that run together like ties on the tail of a kite; let me soar with utter abandon on the whispered wings of the wind of your love. *Amen.*

## ~ Tuesday ~

O Lord,

Quiet this restless anxiety that crawls around the edges of my frailty. Dust it off with a wisp of your heavenly breath, infusing into me the serenity and quietude that my whole being longs for. Talk to me, talk to me in silence, as if your whole presence is testifying on my behalf…that I am worth defending against the lies of self doubt, that I am worth loving. Present me with the gift of the present and take away my anxious need to borrow the worry and troubles from tomorrow. Fill me with your assurance that you will be by my side forever, that you will not lose me, not now, not ever. *Amen.*

## ~ *Wednesday* ~

Lord,

Help me curb my tongue when I lash out in fury. Let me turn to your Son Jesus who lived and died as the ultimate sacrifice for the forgiveness of all our sins, and ask him to place the words of forgiveness on my lips, the charity of forgiveness in my heart and the ability to truly move on. Let me leave all bitterness and wrong doing behind in the yesterdays of my life, knowing that to keep bringing them into the present only invites the harbinger of mean and spiteful ways.

Cleanse my mind and heart of this most recent hurt that I have transformed into anger. Take it and wash my whole being in the river of your mercy so that I may learn to walk a little closer to you.

*Amen.*

✂ *Reflection* ✂
*from a guide on my journey*

Dear Father,

Stir up the spirit of truth in me so I may see clearly today. Today, I just say, "Yes!" I will listen to you. Put hope in my dreams and in my mind as I quietly listen. I will not be afraid of your truth. Light my path and heal my spirit.

Amen.

## ~ Thursday ~

Father God,

I have known physical exhaustion but the exhaustion that comes from mental anguish exacts a huge price on the body. Help me believe that as my body has weakened and tired that my soul has strengthened and taken in the energy of your love. Please show me how to continue waiting in patience.

For what you have said that you would do, I believe that you will. Heal this mind and body which have become so disarranged that I hardly recognize myself some days. Help me visualize your hands holding me, fortifying me with your perfect touch so that I may once again think without fear, act without panic and praise your name from morning to night.

Thank you for this beautiful "Land of the midnight sun;" let me soak in the fragrance of chokecherry blossom, bathe in the essence of lavender growing at my door, and enliven my mind with the striking scent of peppermint as I linger in the garden of my herbs. Be with me tonight as I sleep. Give me dreams of peace and gentleness, be as the dream catcher to snare all unsettling night visions and help me wake alive and refreshed.

*Amen.*

### ⟨ *Reflection* ⟩

*Abba, catch my dreams tonight; turn them in your hand so that their gentle side is revealed and I awake with gratitude and praise on my lips.*

## ~ *Friday* ~

Abba,

If I wait to trust you until all is right with me will I have learned anything through this long dark night? Summer unfolds around me with foliage and color and fragrance. If there were no creator, how could there be such perfection in creation? I gaze into the bloom of a rose and see such infinite tenderness in the design; I smell the headiness of plumeria that diffuses into the tropical night, and I know without a doubt that your hand has touched the smallest detail. How then could I have any doubt that you would stand by me, walk with me, and watch over me through this long dark winter that has overshadowed spring and now blossoms into summer. My heart reaches out for the wellspring that Moses created with his staff. A miracle born for my thirsty soul. *Amen.*

### ⤝ *Reflection* ⤞

Abba,

When the fear magnifies every symptom of suffering, I stop and breathe in faith the sweetest lightest aroma the heavens sprinkle on earth. When the aloneness closes in, catching me unprepared, I call on the name of the Lord.

O my Abba,

Forgive me my shortcomings for I have let go of your hand and I now feel lost and alone. Stay with me tonight as I grasp your hand more firmly, as I pray my prayers more earnestly. I ask you to show me gentleness when I fall, to pick me up tenderly. Bathe me with the salt of heavenly tears. This has been such a long and difficult struggle.

To wait in patience has been the task you have asked of me, and I have done poorly at times.

Set my sails so that they might catch the wind of your breath; strengthen my compass that lies within my heart where you have placed it. Help me reach deep and open my heart to that "safe place" where I meet with you in silence. I ask you to give me the right amount of strength, at the very moment I need it.

Help me not worry about tomorrow's troubles or sorrows, for you will fortify me with what I need when tomorrow comes.

Help me to sail on your wind, whether in stormy seas or in calm waters, knowing that you have placed within me cargo so precious that you will ensure I reach port safely.

Please remember all people tonight who are suffering, even more so than I, for your compassion is limitless.

In your Holy Son's name,
*Amen.*

## ~ Sunday ~

Abba,

Never let me forget to praise you and give you thanks. Let me listen more closely for your whisper woven into birdsong and cathedral bells; let me look more closely for the touch of your hand on all flowers in bloom, on all children at play.

Watching the thunderclouds move across the sky, as first they darken then open with sweet rain, let me hear your mighty voice in the peals of thunder as you call each of us to the story of salvation. A simple story of faith full of more power than we can imagine. I am in awe of all you have done for me. How could anyone turn away from your Holy name? Your handprint on this creation is so distinct that not one of us mortals should fail to see its indelible mark. Open my heart to your limitless love.

In Christ's name,

*Amen.*

## ~ Monday ~

Abba,

Hand me your God-given grace so that I may turn my anger into forgiveness. Let me bury deeply all woundedness and waves of injustice. I shall plant grass as green as the hillsides in spring over this unmarked grave. I will leave my sorrow to be transformed into the sweet blossoms of the apple tree, and I will transcend this earthly hurt, for *Love covers over all wrongs.* Proverbs 10:12

*Amen.*

## ~ Tuesday ~

Abba,

My body has leaned on you for so long that I am imprinted with your serenity. For now that is sufficient and a great reward for my patience. I cried out and you heard me. You sent Angels to be placed directly in my path so that I would say "Yes Lord, yes Lord, yes, yes Lord."

Come be with me, your warm and gracious hand over my heart, stilling all life to the gentle ebb and flow of the tide that changes not.

*Amen.*

## ~ Wednesday ~

Abba,

Smooth the slightly ragged edges of the circle of my mind. Let it turn, without cracks, let it open without breaks, let it learn without resentment. Fill me with your ever present love.

*Amen.*

## ⊂ Reflection ⊃

*Silence. Teach me to sit in silence, my ear to the heartbeat of God, learning to listen to the answers of questions not yet asked.*

## ~ *Thursday* ~

Abba,

The dark face of discouragement has camped upon my heart and I feel waves of despair as I struggle with the not knowing. The not knowing of when or if this illness will pass, the not knowing if I will regain my mental and physical strength. Help me lay down the spear of fear, for if I carry it, it will only pierce my heart again and again. Lay upon me the cloak that you made for me in heaven, even before I came into this body. Help me understand that this cloak is all encompassing, all strengthening and all protecting. It is made of the finest gossamer web, but it carries your rich and powerful voice praying for the strength of a thousand chariot horses, to carry me safely through the channels of this dark black sea.

Be with me tonight with your hand upon my heart so that I know I am not navigating alone.

*Amen.*

## ✄ *Reflection* ✄

*Lift your eyes and look to the heavens: who created all these? He who brings out the starry host one by one, and calls them each by name. Because of his great power and mighty strength, not one of them is missing.* Isaiah 40:26

## ~ Friday ~

*"My soul is in anguish. How long, O LORD, how long?"*
Psalm 6: 3

Keep me loving and praising you O Lord, for great things will be asked of those who have been given much. The mystery of faith is just that…isn't it…a mystery in how long we must wait, a mystery in knowing what answer we will receive. Keep me focused only on all that is positive in my world knowing that my body is on loan from you, that my soul willingly filled this body when you asked, "Who can bear great pain and suffering, if it will bring praise to my name and comfort to many?"

Help me not to ask, "What if God doesn't heal me?" Rather, help me ask "What if God knows that at his appointed time, one of my prayers will save someone's life? And yet I will never know."

Love me, hold me, escort me through this "valley of the shadow of death"; take all fear from my heart and replace it with faith.

*Amen.*

### ∝ *Reflection* ∝

*We live by faith, not by sight.* 2 Corinthians 5:7

## ~ *Saturday* ~

Abba,

Night has been turned into day; my eyes have been swollen shut with crying, now they have been opened. I give you thanks from the inner sanctum of my spirit where we have met so many lonely nights; where you have helped me wrestle my demons, where, when I have fallen weak and prostrated myself on the empty cell of my soul, you have picked up my armor and fought for me. Yes, you have fought for me.

For all the times that I have believed that I was not worth fighting for, you have proved me wrong. You have stood by my side at every turn of the battle; you have shouted my name in victory and you have given me purpose to live.

Bless my doctors and all helpers for believing in me. Help me to continue to take one day at a time, knowing there will be rocky times ahead. But for now, for these good days in the sunshine of your green pastures, I am full of gratitude that you have graced me with still waters.

Thank you my Father.

Help me to be worthy of your fight for me.

*Amen.*

## *- Sunday -*

Abba, my dear Abba,

Although this is the last prayer I set into print, I will never cease to praise your name and to thank you for all you have done for me. You have led me through the most troublesome tempest, you have sheltered me in the pelting rain, you have fed me with the warmth of your healing, and you have cast my anchor into the steadfast floor of the sea. There is no way to repay you for your works of plenty, and yet there is no need, as you have offered all this to me in the name of Grace, which Jesus bestowed upon us all as he died on the cross for us. Help me to live as the woman you have made me, help me love, as you have loved me.

In the name of your precious Son, Jesus Christ,
*Amen.*

While Jesus was standing there, he cried out, Let anyone who is thirsty come to me, and let the one who believes in me drink. As the scripture has said, Out of the believer's heart shall flow rivers of living water. John 7:37-38 NRSV

*Amen.*

## ⋈ *My Reflections* ⋈

*⤳ My Reflections ⤝*

*My Reflections*

*My Reflections*

Ichthus or ichthys is the Greek word meaning fish. The five Greek letters that spell ichthus, $IX\Theta Y\Sigma$, stand for the words meaning Jesus Christ, Son of God, Savior. Christians in the early church years used the ichthus symbol to identify or acknowledge a fellow believer in Christ. In order to prevent capture and persecution Christians would draw an ichthus in the dirt, mud, sand, or on cave walls to let another Christian know that it was safe to talk about their faith without the fear of being turned in.

### ~ With Gratitude ~

As part of this ongoing journey, I thank all my spirit sisters and brothers who have helped me with this book. I especially thank Linda for her loving support and manuscript design.

~ Peggy

I welcome your comments and stories.
You may email me at peggyjmcmahon@gmail.com

*In Memory of Shana Weber*